Made in United States
Orlando, FL
10 February 2022

14682156R00068